AF243712

Love and Life

Cedar Leaf Press
17503 La Cantera Pkwy, #104-240
San Antonio, TX 78257

Library of Congress Cataloging-in-Publication Data

Christophersen, D. J. [date]

Love and Life: Celebrated in Poems and Aphorisms

p.   cm.

ISBN   978-0-9820413-7-6 (paper)

Library of Congress Control Number: 2010921166

1. Christophersen, D. J. [date]. 2. Poetry—Love.
3. Poetry—Animals. 4. Poetry—Life. 5. Aphorisms.

Printed in the United States of America
Printed on acid-free paper

Love and Life

Celebrated in Poems and Aphorisms

D. J. Christophersen

Cedar Leaf Press
San Antonio, Texas

Writ with pleasure
Beyond measure
For my lovely wife,
Who, like no other,
Helped me discover
Meaning in this life

Contents

Contents

Part Three: Life in This World

Part Four: Aphorisms

Contents

Part One

Romantic Love

True Love

Let me not by the mystery of true love be unmoved.
For what the famous bard has writ is naught but proved—
"Love is not love that alters when it alteration finds."
By these pure words as needles sure
Are brought together two far minds
Before uncolored and uncommon plain—
Two hearts now knit and purled from a single skein
That cannot be unraveled by thorns of strife
Nor other snares and brambles of this encumbered life.
Seamless throughout love will not tear,
Neither spot nor wrinkle does it bear.
And though with time all other garments sure will fade,
Love alone is for the ages made.
When all else fails true love will last.
True love's colors are made fast.
Love's not a fashion that with season varies.
But love, true love, renews the minds it marries.
If by these words I somehow error show,
May I and all the world without love's garment go.

I Love You

I love you. . .
When the twilight willingly surrenders
Itself to the arms of evening,
When the youthfulness of evening
Grows to the maturity of midnight,
When the strength of night
Weakens to the frailness of dawn,
When the broken morning stretches
To the madness of midday,
When the day walks softly
In the shadows of the afternoon,
When the waning sun lays its
Withering hand on the shoulder of dusk,
I love you. . .
I love you. . .
I love you. . .

My Time With You

Today I think of you,
Not less than yesterday.
Today I think of you,
Traveling on your way.
Today I think of you
As you go out the door.
Today I think of you
And love you more and more.
Tomorrow is another day,
I'll miss your being here.
Tomorrow is another day,
I'll always hold you dear.
Tomorrow is another day,
My heart is in your hand.
Tomorrow is another day,
Just knowing you is grand.
The past is but a memory,
A history of our days.

Romantic Love

The past is but a memory,
A roadmap of our ways.
The past is but a memory,
That makes us what we are.
The past is but a memory,
Though we be near or far.
The future is our happiness,
I'll love you through the years.
The future is our happiness,
Our hopes dispel our fears.
The future is our happiness,
Our blessings are not few.
The future is our happiness,
It's all because of you.
Today I give you all my love,
There's nothing more to give.
Today I give you all my love
For as long as I shall live.
Today I give you all my love,
Let earth my witness be.
Today I give you all my love
Throughout eternity.

Missing You

So far the distance us divides
And close these walls enfold
The emptiness that now abides,
If all the truth be told.
Without your presence gently by,
Your voice to fill the air,
The moments all but fleeting fly
The day is all but fair.
Time lumbers on so slow of pace
And pauses oft to stand
In silence watching for your face
And waiting for your hand.
Could I but gain a furtive glance
And catch your smiling eye,
So spritely would my spirit dance
Beneath a cloudless sky.
It is the little things I miss.
I cannot say how much—

Romantic Love

The way you move, the gentle kiss,
The tempo of your touch.
If time should grant us added grace,
Though we be here or there,
Whatever comes cannot replace
The memories that we share.
And so I wait while minutes pass
And turn themselves to hours,
And know that hope will soon surpass
Time's unrestricted powers.
And then your wondrous face I'll see,
Your beauty I'll behold.
These ponderous moments all shall flee
When you my arms enfold.

The Perfect Gift

Could I the substance
Of your love enfold,
The farthest reaches
Of your mind unfold,
The beauty of your heart
And face be told,
Let time be stopped
And wonder take its place.
What gift is there that I could bring
To satisfy your smile?
Is there created product made
To fully match your style?
Mere things to buy or time to take
To walk another mile?
Let all remove
And you alone replace.
Another year, another measure
Of the time we share,

Romantic Love

Another chance to stand aside
And let you know I care,
What can I do to really show
The length and breadth of love
That you alone will always have
From me, my sweetheart dove?
You are my peace, my olive branch,
The pulse of what I do.
There is no joy, no sense of worth
Apart from knowing you.
You are my breath, my sight, my touch,
The longing of my heart.
You are the essence of the space
Of which I am a part.
With you I've found the fullness
Of a life I never knew.
Whatever I have now become
Is all because of you.
I cannot say what might have been.
I cannot ever know
What hides behind the future
In events that come and go.
But of this one thing I am sure,
As sure as I can be,

Love and Life

You are the best, the only one,
God's perfect gift for me.
Let no material gift reflect
The beauty of this thought:
Let nothing ever take the place
Of love alone that ought
To be the sole and constant energy
To take us through each day,
To move us farther down the road,
To guide us on the way.
Let love between us ever grow
And make us purely one,
To be together always
Like the Father and the Son.
Another year will come and go,
And then a hundred more,
And from this world we both shall pass
To enter heaven's door.
I cannot think of greater bliss
Than on that other shore
To have you there beside me
In love forevermore.

Two Loves

I.

Being with you this night
Has placed within my life
A sense of awe and deep
Regard for what one moment,
An island in time, can do to
Make an otherwise normal
And ordinary life sublime.
To feel your touch, your warm embrace,
To look upon your angel face,
To see your smile in lips and eyes,
To have you take me by surprise
To a warm and tender quiet spot,
Where love is long and time is not,
And then to be with you as one
As night gives way to the morning sun,
In this I find my spirit soars
Beyond the known to open doors

Love and Life

Where nobles brave might fear to stand
While I less brave would enter grand
A vast expanse of world before
Though on my knees.

II.

Yes, on my knees, in soul and heart,
Because this time is but a part
Of God's great plan for one who hears
With other ears the voice of love,
Which takes no form but of the Dove
Who sits upon the window sill
Of every life and speaks to those
Who take the time to listen—
To listen and to hear that gentle voice
Dispel the fear that sometimes grips the heart
Of those who walk alone with groping hands:
"Come my child, up from your knees,
Do not have fear and if you please,
Come fly with me to know the joy
Of beauty shared and multiplied—
Come take my hand!"

Anniversary

I.

Alone I sat to break my fast
With eggs and toast and coffee last.
Alone and incomplete was I
Like earth without the sun in sky.
Man is not made to live alone.
His wife is called bone of his bone.
Together they become as one,
Just like the earth around the sun.
The orbits that they took before
Are not their circles anymore.
Poetry cannot describe
The universe they circumscribe.
For when a man has found his mate,
All other women do not rate.
His heart is by her beauty won,
Again just like the earth and sun
He travels round what she desires,

Love and Life

His heart aflame with glowing fires
Fanned by love and pure devotion,
As though he'd drunk some magic potion.
He serves her needs without debate,
Always early, never late.
She wants to know he loves her only.
He in turn is never lonely.

II.

About our journey since we met,
That day I never shall forget,
A lengthy book I might have written—
I am so deeply by you smitten,
But I shall have to cut it short.
There's too much history now to sort.
Twenty-five years have just gone by.
You're sun, I'm earth, and in our sky
We travel daily Love's true line,
For I am yours and you are mine.
There's really nothing more to say
On this our anniversary day.
Let love between us ne'er depart.
You are my all, my dear sweetheart.

Standing By

For every challenge that you face,
For every memory you can trace,
For every hope that you embrace,
For every step you take apace,
You'll find that I am standing by.

For every dream that will come true,
For every work you have to do,
For every sky from gray to blue,
For every burden known by few,
You'll find that I am standing by.

For every day you have a care,
For every task you need to share,
For every load you have to bear,
For every place no matter where,
You'll find that I am standing by.

For every song that you will sing,
For every joy each day will bring,

Love and Life

For every thought that's on the wing,
For every single living thing,
You'll find that I am standing by.

For every moment that you live,
For every gift that life can give,
For every error that you forgive,
For every hurt that you outlive,
You'll find that I am standing by.

For every goal that you achieve,
For every wish that you conceive,
For every creed that you believe,
For every loss that you retrieve,
You'll find that I am standing by.

For every day that is begun,
For every mile that you must run,
For every victory that's won,
For every thing that makes us one,
You'll find that I am standing by.

The Meeting

When many generations had passed
And the wind had blown clear
The landscape of their memories and dreams,
They stood there alone together
As one silhouette against the sky,
Eyes interlocked,
Their gazes painting their own
Portraits on the single canvas
Of their lives.
They who had been together
Since eternity began
Were meeting now for the first time.
They did not speak.
There was no one to hear.

Cancer

I.

I was sensate then, before the call,
But now am numb and that is all.
There was more of me before somehow,
But I am so diminished now.
Would that I could take your pain—
Your loss so easily made my gain.
In love all other things we share,
But this alone I'd gladly bear.
If only I could set you free—
No other thought can comfort me.
What are you that I should care?
Nothing but the very air I breathe.
Surely at this time of greatest test
I know that I am the most blessed.
I cannot count the many ways
You fill the hours of all my days.
In my darkness you are light.

Romantic Love

In my blindness you are sight.
In my sadness you are song.
In my weakness you are strong.
If I were Sheol, you'd be heaven.
If I were bread, you'd be leaven.
When skies are gray and the way is weary,
Just your voice can make me cheery.
In every trial you are hope.
When I am drowning you are rope.
You have a sunny disposition
And wisdom too for those who listen.
You are a prefect work of art,
And I have loved you from the start.

II.

Now our month of trial is over,
And I am like a cow in clover.
Content at last and anxious free,
I wondered if I'd ever be.
Successful surgery's now completed.
Cancer cells are all defeated.
Not one malignancy's discovered.
Now we wait till you're recovered.
A scar remains a tale to tell

Love and Life

That you are now completely well—
A testimony to your care
And courage where there was despair.
The future now looks very bright.
Your hopes and dreams are all in sight.
Your loved ones standing by are true.
There's nothing we won't do for you.
Each prayer we've made has had its answer.
We're glad to know you're free of cancer.
Let peace supreme reign in your heart,
And nevermore your joy depart.

My Valentine

Come dance with me, my lovely bride,

And with each step let love abide

Within our hearts forever more

While we are dancing to the score

Of life's sweet music in our ears.

Let joy be ours and through the years

May all that is be yours and mine—

My sweet, beloved valentine!

Love's Invitation

Come to me, my eternal love,
As the summer rains to thirsty soils—
Come to me.

As the deer comes to the water's edge
To quench a day-long thirst—
Come to me.

On the wings of the eagle
Soaring high in the cloudless sky,
In the freedom of the eagle—
Come to me.

In summer on the sheet of rain
Driven on the open sea by the power of the wind,
In the very objects carried by the foaming surf
That divides the continents—
Come to me.

Romantic Love

In the gentle rains, my love,
In the freedom of the eagle,
In the cautious silence of the thirsty doe,
In the stormy sea—
Come to me, my eternal love.

Part Two

Love for Animals

The Mite and I

Not unlike some other rhymers,
Painters of words, and syntax timers,
I too have seen the paper mite,
Lowly esteemed on fields of white.
Like his fellows born of eggs,
He's far too small to see his legs.
But give him paper and a notion,
And off he goes in frenzied motion.
He scurries through the territory
Completely mindless of the story
That I develop beneath his feet.
My thoughts are nothing but his street.
Not one word does he inspect,
While I, conversely, pause to reflect
On every movement that he makes
Upon my progress or mistakes.
My intent is not to kill him.
I much prefer that I might thrill him

Love for Animals

With some pithy statement wise
Or thoughts of somewhat smaller size.
But these are not his destination.
He seems bent on mastication.
If only he would concentrate—
Meditate not ambulate—
He might devour some juicy thought
Beyond the morsel that he sought.
It's clear our purposes don't jibe,
But somehow we're still both alive
To serve the means by which we go.
And if you really want to know,
In the end we're much alike.
I write some words; he takes a hike.
What we do is just a caper.
The mite and I, we run on paper.

Elegy to Libra

Some felines are just average cats.
By nature they will search out rats,
But more than that they cannot do.
No one can say the same for you.
For you're far above the usual run
Of cats that people have for fun.
Smarter, like an engineer,
You often brought your parents cheer.
I recall the day we met.
On that great day our fate was set.
You and Luna came for good,
Came to change our livelihood.
Until that day twelve years ago,
We had no pets that we could know.
Our view of life was narrow then.
You broadened us beyond our ken.
We watched you grow and in our hearts
We learned we had some missing parts.

Love for Animals

Before, we did just as we pleased,
Until we met the Siamese.
Your gentle and persistent ways
Became the benchmark of our days.
We never saw you lose your cool,
And clearly you were no one's fool.
Proud and stubborn some would say,
But patient as the livelong day.
In pain we never heard you cry,
Though many times we wondered why.
It's hard to say how much we learned,
But everything to which you turned,
And everything you came to touch
Bequeathed to us so very much.
Too quickly through our lives you passed.
The days and years flew by too fast.
And though you've gone to higher ground,
The ache within our heart's profound.
We wish that we could see your face
From this forlorn and empty place.
But now you're gone and we remain,
Amd we will never be the same.
You were special like the showers
Bringing life to wilting flowers.

Love and Life

Tender heart and constant friend,
You'll be with us to the end.
No one else can take your place.
Within our hearts you'll find a space
To live forever as you will,
A space that nothing else can fill.
Where you are now we cannot go,
But on your journey travel slow,
For one day we shall follow on
And join you when our day is done.
Until that day we hope you wait
Close as you can to heaven's gate.
And as all souls pass by that door,
We too shall cross to heaven's shore.
And then together we shall go
Forever on and always know
That what we had upon this earth
Was just the start of endless worth.
So now, dear Libra, go in peace,
Free from pain, free to release
Your charm to all who pass your way
And, like us, they're sure to say
That knowing you has made them blessed
In special ways beyond the rest.

Love for Animals

And so, although our ways shall part,
We'll take you with us in our heart.
Goodbye, dear Libra, friend, goodbye.
We hurt because you had to die.
But deep within this awful strife,
We have our hope in eternal life.
We know that you are still alive,
And hope constrains us to survive
With happy thoughts of times we had,
Though now we are so very sad.
Greet all our friends on the other side,
Our family too where they abide.
And we shall hold our heads up high
And always keep your memory nigh.

Ode To Max

When the clouds of sorrow darken
Skies above of royal blue,
When our broken hearts surrender
Everything that's good and true,
When our muddled minds consider
That the best for us to do
Is to let the heavy burdens
Ruin all the hope we knew—
That is when we need each other
To believe that all's not dross.
That is when we need our faith
To cover all, despite the loss.
That is when hope will sustain us
Though the billows round us toss.
That is when our love must guide us
Over every bridge we cross.
When this time of grief is over,
Then one day we'll sing again.

Love for Animals

But today our song is silenced
Shrouded by a veil of pain.
Still we know that we are victors,
Stronger daily as we gain
Strength in weakness now unmeasured
As we travel through this strain.
Joy will come that distant morning
When we see your boyish face,
When our hearts are light with laughter,
As we come to share your space.
Stand by, dear friend, just watch and wait
For we'll be coming sure of pace.
Stand by till then and rest assured
That no one else can take your place.

Diva's Song

Night surrounds me black as coal.
The pangs of death torment my soul.
The loss of Diva takes its toll
Upon my troubled mind.
How can it be at four weeks old
We find her lifeless body cold,
Her outstretched limbs the story told
Of far too much exhaustion?
Why did she have to die so young?
Her song was never fully sung.
The syllables upon her tongue
Were only baby cries.
I cannot stop the flood of tears.
They're not a fountain of my fears,
But of the hopes of many years
I might have had with her.
Although the time is barely past
When little Diva breathed her last,

Love for Animals

Like molten iron fully cast
This lesson I have learned:
It's not how long we live this life,
In joy and laughter grief and strife—
The truth cuts through me like a knife—
It's what we have to give.
What Diva gave was in her face,
Her big, round eyes a strong embrace
Of trust and every good and grace
This world will ever know.
The song that Diva had to sing
Forever in my ears shall ring,
For her it was the only thing.
Her song was in her eyes.

Cirrus the Cat

If you only knew the work I do
When you leave this hallowed hall.
You think I play, I guess you'd say.
Well, sir, do you have gall!
Who counts the time from six till nine,
Or whenever you get home?
Oh, you think it's great to stay out late.
Well, it's hard to be alone!
And it takes a while (I thought you'd smile)
To do the things I do.
Like who puts hair on every chair?
Cirrus the cat—that's who!
It's a funny thing, if cats could sing,
You'd have me at the Met.
But since I won't (not saying I don't),
I'm just your average pet.
But am I upset like your average pet
Whenever things go wrong?

Love for Animals

You bet I'm not, 'cuz what you've got
Is a cat that lives a song.
If a dog had my place, it'd be a disgrace.
He'd probably be delirious.
But who keeps his cool and is never the fool?
Cirrus the cat—the serious!
Now I'm done with this rhyme,
'Cuz I'm fresh out of time,
And I've other things to do—
Like sit and reflect
And think on respect
For Cirrus the cat—that's who!

Beavers and Birches

I.

When I see stock tanks scattered here and there
Across the Texas landscape vast and fair,
I like to think some beaver's been building them,
But beavers do not build these ponds.
Ranchers do that.
Often you must have seen them
Driving their pickups,
A sunny summer morning during a drought.
They rise up early as the new day breaks
And ride the range from tank to tank
Inspecting cattle.
Soon they park their F350's and mount their dozers,
Moving and grading great piles of earth.
Such heaps of broken earth to rearrange,
You'd think the whole of Texas needed grading.
The tanks are shaped and reshaped by the dozers
And they are meant not to leak;

Love for Animals

But unless a base of clay is laid,
They most assuredly will.
You may see their waterless craters
Dotting the Texas landscape years afterward,
Mocking the rancher's cattle that hope to find
Within their empty bowls
The smallest drop of water to slake their thirst.

II.

But I was going to say when Truth broke in
With all her matter-of-fact about the ranchers,
I should prefer to have some beavers build them
The way they do in Wisconsin,
Whose expertise in building is widely known,
Spring, summer, and autumn before the freeze.
One by one they subdue the forest trees
By chewing them down bite by bite
Until at last the trees are felled.
And not one is hung up.
Not one is left for them to conquer.
They know instinctively all there is to know
About where to chew so as to fell the tree
Exactly where they want it.
They always plan to fell the tree precisely

Love and Life

Where the dam will make the stream
Fill the pond up to the brim,
And even above the brim.
Then they stand back and the tree falls
With a swish,
Crashing its way down
Through the air
To the ground.

III.

So was I once myself a watcher of beavers,
And so I dream of going back to be.
It's when I feel like Robert Frost
And life is like the pathless wood
He so eloquently describes.
And cobwebs and snares entrap
Even the most valiant efforts of the mind
To achieve serenity.
I'd like to get away from earth for a while, too,
And, like Frost,
Have a second chance at everything.
And I also hope that nothing,
Whether fate or fortune,
Might grant my wish

Love for Animals

And snatch me away from my dreams.
Earth's the right place for love,
It's true.
But that's not all.
It's the right place for watching beavers, too,
Absorbed in the silent observation
Of master builders
As they do what they do best,
Until one could watch no more,
Until the waning twilight
Embraces the warm breast of night.
That would be good
No matter how you look at it.
One could do worse than be a watcher of beavers.

Part Three

Life in This World

This World Is Not for Me

I.

This world is not for me.
Too much is told of greed and gain
By those who are the source of pain,
While other voices saying more
Can fain be heard amidst the roar
Of endless clamoring and war
For more of nothingness.

II.

This world is not for me
When truth is lost amidst the din
Of crime without and lies within
And justice waits upon its knees
As if to beg with silent pleas
To be released from the tyrannies
Of more of nothingness.

Life in This World

III.

This world is not for me,
If such there be whose lives are lost
To siege and war at any cost
And hungry mouths still go unfed
While rats and worms consume the bread
Which might have rescued those now dead
From more of nothingness.

IV.

This world is not for me,
For love which fills the deepest heart
Cannot be shared by those apart,
Though solitude need not despoil
The silence as the fertile soil
Where true love grows, not in the toil
For more of nothingness.

V.

This world is not for me,
Unless there be with all the noise
Some laughter and the pleasant joys

Love and Life

Of silent walks on moonlit sands,
Of tender smiles and gentle hands
Which pull asunder all the bands
Of more of nothingness.

Ode to a Rose

Shades of crimson stand cool and silhouetted.
Dewy memories of the night linger as beads of crystal
On tender petals,
Resting as caresses on gentle hands.
Sensuous.
Silent yet beckoning, perched as a sentinel of splendor on an
Emerald pillar
Waiting on the wings of morning
To show yourself a beauty queen—
Who of all the flowers stands your equal,
Thou fairest of the
Arboretum?

My Friend the Sea

When I go down to the sea at night,
To listen to her voice,
She questions me
With "Are you free?"
And "Can you make a choice?"
"There is a place," she says to me,
"Where you can truly silent be.
And only there within that spot
Can you be free to choose your lot.
It is not far for you to go,
As surely as the night winds blow,
But go you must and when you do
The God of peace will be with you."
She sows these words within my heart
And says that I must do my part
If ever I should like to be
As vast and peaceful as the sea.
When I go down to the sea at night

Life in This World

To watch the billows roll,
The rhythm of the foaming surf
Becomes the music of my soul.
We are good friends, the sea and I,
Who let our friendship grow
In little ways that are not forced,
Ways never done for show.
She brings me gifts from time to time
And leaves them on the sand:
A yellow piece of plastic
Or a Pepsi Cola can.
She loves to give, my friend the sea,
I never have to plead.
And always when she brings me things,
They're exactly what I need.

Character

Far to the north in this fair land,
Far from the mountains and ocean strand
Where winter is long and summer short
And rivers stream to some far port,
Where forests verdant blanket hills
Till autumn leaf with color fills
The eye with beauty utmost fair,
Then leaves the trees completely bare—
There in the north woods I have found
That character is in the ground,
For from the soil all things are drawn.
With toil its timber logs are sawn.
In summer fields of grain are grown,
But not till rocks from glaciers sown
Have been removed by plow or hand
In efforts to redeem the land.
Trees and rocks a picture make—
But not in fields for goodness' sake!

Life in This World

The work is hard and long the days
To mend the course of nature's ways.
With rocks and trees she meant no harm,
But she wasn't thinking of the farm.
Nor did she have in mind the reason
For making short the growing season.
Yet truth be told without restraint,
The farmer voices no complaint.
He does his duties dry or wet
Within the bounds the soil has set.
He clears his fields and grows his grain
And very often for no gain,
But he feeds his family well enough
And keeps on going though it's tough.
And with each year he wiser grows
Because above all else he knows
That what he has his hands have earned,
Though many pleasures he has spurned.
His own desires he puts aside,
And so he lifts his head with pride.
His character from work is made
With horse or tractor plow or spade.
And when his modest work is done,
He knows he's fought the soil and won.

Smog Basin

Smog basin, smog basket,
Smog basin, smog casket.
Progress made it smell this way.
At home, at work and when we play
We fill our lungs at every breath
With hydrocarbons, smoke, and death.
Stately mountains rim this basin,
But they never have a place in
What we do from day to day,
And not because they're far away.
Their glorious heights cannot be seen
Through air that's orange or ghastly green.

Flying

Part of flying is the waiting,
Sitting still, anticipating.
Nothing else is there to do
But sit and think of skies of blue.
"Like a blanket is the fog,"
Writes the captain in his log.
He thinks of family far away
And hopes to end this dreary day.
The passengers, relaxed and seated,
Coffee hot to them is meted.
They're calm about the flight that's pending,
Or is it that they're just pretending?
The crew, like nurses, tend their patients
With pillows, blankets, and other maintenance.
Stoics used to such delays say
"This is just another day."
All of us for different reasons
Migrate like the birds in seasons.

Love and Life

And like them we cannot say
What motivates us in this way.
But the best we think we're doing
So we wait for flights ensuing,
Trusting in Bernoulli's law
To transport us without a flaw.
At last the tower gives us clearance.
The weather's now no interference.
"Cleared to taxi to the runway,"
Means that we can start our day.
We soon forget the minutes wasted.
Breakfast now we all have tasted.
Soaring in our situation,
Nothing is like aviation!

Taxes

Taxes are not something that relaxes.
Rendering money unto Caesar
May be good for the believer,
But Uncle Sam is not a miser.
Often he could be much wiser
In the way he spends our dough.
We could do with less for show
And more for better enterprises—
Less for projects in disguises.
We see barrels fat with pork
And not the kind consumed with fork,
But waste that's far beyond compare—
Beyond what most of us can bear.
Unless our heads are in the sand,
Sam's budget simply isn't planned.
Let's take an easy, bold example.
Let's go where only fools will trample
And talk about the military.

Love and Life

Now there's a subject really hairy.
Who knows where our money goes?
Where is the bottom line that shows
Our dimes and nickels have been counted?
Our dollars into piles are mounted.
Congress comes to sit in place.
Generals come to make their case.
Such great minds all come together,
See our cash and like a feather
Windy bureaucrats blow our money.
Really this is not so funny.
Just imagine if they earned it,
Worked by day and night and churned it
Out the way we do.
Perhaps then there would be a few
Who'd pause a moment before they spent
The pile of money that we sent.
Taxes are not something that relaxes.

Silence

Silence speaks to those who,
Like the morning roses,
Have the dew as
Their nectar.
Here there is no subject apart,
Nor object of separateness,
Nor ears to hear
Or understand.
Here the voice of Silence cries out,
"Awake, O sleeper, it is
Morning on a new day.
It is for you."

Friendship

Like the ocean, let your friendship be
Vast enough for endless exploration,
Deep enough to hide personal treasures,
Open enough to admit discovery,
Strong enough to move the immovable,
Playful enough to elicit laughter,
Peaceful enough to personify tranquility,
Wild enough to remain unpredictable,
Secret enough to speak in whispers,
Free enough to kiss the wind and be moved.
Like the ocean, let your friendship be.

Too Late

Nothing

Now have I to say

That cannot wait

For another

Day.

The Commute

Look at all

The people going

To and fro upon the earth,

Steeled and glassed

In boxes rolling,

Calculating

What it's

Worth.

The Trail of Life

I.

I shall not pass this way again.
The road is winding sore.
Its hazards mark my every step,
Its narrowness far more.
Behind I see the lights of home
Where comforts more abound
And turn an empty ear that way
To hear sweet voices sound.
But silent is the pathway now
and dim the darkening wood,
While on the trail my feet gain not
In progress toward the good.
Astray I come to find this path
Of sorrow and of shame,
Where countless others lost their way

Love and Life

And sacrificed their name.
What course they took to this bleak place
I can in vain scarce tell,
Nor in my state so desolate
Care I to wish them well.
To self alone I turn my thoughts
And find there's nothing there—
No light, no love, no gentleness
No tenderness to share.
It is alone I grope my way
And press on without hope.
My cause forsaken, blind am I—
I stumble on the slope.
Too steep it goes and greatly high—
I have not strength or will
To gain a foothold sure and safe
Upon this endless hill.

II.

And then, behold, a flash of light
Expels the darkness of my night.
And suddenly the way seems clear,
And I without the former fear
Am energized by some new power.

Life in This World

Recovering like a withered flower
Fed and nurtured and renewed,
With life afresh I am embued.
I rise with shoulders held square back.
My pace is quickened without slack.
The trail though narrow still seems wide
As I emboldened lengthen stride.
And marching on the lighted way
I find somehow the words to say
To fellow travelers in their sorrow:
"Do not despair, for bright tomorrow
Has a store of hope for one
Whose eyes in faith behold the Son.
Do not walk alone, my friend.
Do not struggle to the end,
For God will meet your every need,
Though faith be small as mustard seed.
Look up, look to the light ahead.
Set not your gaze on where you tread.
The roadmap to the path you travel
Is not written in the gravel.
Look up, take heart, and set your eyes
Upon the Son who fills the skies
With all the brightness of his face

To guide you safely through the race,
To offer you a share of grace,
To lead you to that final place
Where in his presence you will find
Eternal joy and peace of mind."

The Storm

Dawn woke worn and weary.
The sky hung low and gray.
The air was damp and dreary
On a sullen, sunless day.
The hours passed foreboding,
Portending things to come,
As darkening clouds were loading,
Filling to the maximum.
We battened down the hatches,
Windows shuttered not to break,
The doors secured with latches,
In our cabin by the lake.
By afternoon the air had cooled.
The birds no longer winging
Nested warm, they were not fooled,
And all had stopped their singing.
A tactile stillness gripped the air.
The sky seemed closer still.

Love and Life

The calm we knew was cause for care.
We felt a sudden chill.
The storm clouds gathered in the east
And, billowing and black,
Took on the image of a beast
That meant to leave its track.
It roared and flashed its fiery eyes
And pushed the rain before.
In giant strides without disguise,
The bull advanced to gore.
Fast the murderous beast came crashing,
Stirring white caps on the lake—
Pounding, driving, threatening, flashing—
Leaving wreckage in its wake.
The fishermen did not survive.
The wind was much too strong.
Not one of them returned alive.
The bull had done them wrong.
And still not satisfied it blew
With fury mounting higher.
Bold and cruel it roared anew,
Outraged and breathing fire.
By landfall it was freely smashing
Every object in its path—

Life in This World

Slamming, gashing, ripping, bashing—
Hostile in rampaging wrath.
We surrendered to its beating.
Nothing else was there to do,
But to hope the hour was fleeting
When its brutal deeds were through.
The cabin trembled badly shaken,
Creaked and rattled all the more
As, despite our measures taken,
The bull kept banging at the door
And from the roof the shingles stripping.
We rushed for pots and pans
To catch the streams of water dripping—
We soon ran out of cans.
The storm continued through the night,
Unchained and fiercely blowing.
There was no let up to its might,
And then it started snowing.
By morning all the earth was white.
The drifts were piling high.
And still there was no end in sight
To the leaden, ashen sky.
Without a break the snowflakes fell,
A blanket tossed from heaven.

Love and Life

How deep it was we could not tell
Until it stopped at seven.
But then again the rain began
And poured till morning light
And made a crystal wonderland
To everyone's delight.
We left the cabin's warmth at last
And walked upon the snow
Encrusted with a glaze of glass,
The children all in tow.
The crystal snow made not sound.
The air had not a breeze.
The branches bent near to the ground
From ice upon the trees.
Clear and cold the morn remained.
We wandered in the woods.
Our weight the glassy snow sustained—
A solid floor and good.
By noon the sun's warmth could be felt.
It worked its wondrous magic.
And soon the ice began to melt—
In fact we deemed it tragic.
As so we turned to make our way
Back to the cabin small,

Life in This World

And wondered if another day
Could match this one at all.
But from the storm we gathered this—
We learned it to the letter—
Life 's not always filled with bliss
But soon it will get better.

Part Four

Aphorisms

Love and Life

Advice

Do not
Be timid or lax
In the exploration of your
Inner space. Continued examination
Will reveal a vast territory teeming with life
That is unfamiliar to your experience and more
Wonderful that you can imagine now. Do not fear the
Desires of your heart yet unknown to you, and
Do not let the clouds of your thinking
Eclipse the bright sun of
Your feeling.

Aphorisms

Bedtime

My thoughts were all of work today.
It seems there is no other way
Until the lateness of the hour
Directs my soul to a higher power.

Being

Doing is not being.

Birth

Whatever is born is conceived in longing.

Body

There is spirit body and physical body.
The latter is a warden
Of the free-minded spirit
Who would be true to itself
But for the cruel master
Of circumstances that it fears to flee.

Aphorisms

Change

Transition is the place of before and after—
It is the betweenness of the eternal now.

Choices

These narrows
Forced upon me by a foreign hand—
A circumstance I cannot understand—
Have placed me 'tween two choices hard and long.
One choice is right,
The other wrong.
A crossroads this,
And on the way
I choose to either go or stay.

Dance

Dance is movement from the inside out.

Desire

Only one who desires all shall give all.

Aphorisms

Forward

Closer to the mind of God,
A straighter path than I have trod,
Thy word implant within my heart
A new beginning, fresher start.

Home

Home is a place where there is no distance between.

Hope

Hope cannot tell time. It brings the future into now.

Humor

"There is none in the universe,"
said the stoic.
"But it followed me home,"
said the clown.

Aphorisms

Knowledge

The philosopher says, "Know thyself,"
And in so doing falls short of truth in that he would
Conceive of life rather than live it.
Better to have said, "Be thyself."

Learning

Learning is a one-way ticket to where you are not now.

Love and Life

Life

So much life it takes

to fill so small

A

Space

On

Paper

Aphorisms

Love

I.

The name of your beloved

Everywhere on your mind

II.

Your name

Everywhere on the mind

Of your beloved

Pessimism

Two cats went out to play one day

When one was overheard to say,

"I think it's going to rain."

To which the second cat replied,

"I'm sure of it and when it do,

I think it's going to glue."

Aphorisms

Self

Unlike Balaam

We have no donkey

To oppose us—

We stand stubbornly

on our own paths

and oppose

ourselves.

Separation

Time flying on broken wings

Living in a house without windows or doors

Beautiful vistas blindfolded

Vast expanses of distance between one

Vacancy in the midst of fullness

Naught divided and the division multiplied

A portmanteau never forged

Birds and fishes changing places

Iron not attracted to a magnet

Aphorisms

Superpower

Only God

Sympathy

I am you

Love and Life

Time

Time wanders to the edge

Of space

And

Falls

Off

Togetherness

You are butterfly—I am branch.